JETS & PLA

(A Fascinating Book Containing Facts, Trivia, Images & Memory
Recall Quiz: Suitable for Adults & Children)

By

Matthew Harper

For legal reasons we are obliged to state the following:

Hi and a very warm welcome to "Jets & Planes". A Fascinating Book Containing Facts, Trivia, Images & Memory Recall Quiz: Suitable for Adults & Children.

I'm one of those people who loves to hear about extraordinary facts or trivia about anything. They seem to be one of the few things my memory can actually recall. I'm not sure if it's to do with the shock or the "WoW" factor but for some reason my brain seems to store at least some of it for a later date.

I've always been a great believer in that whatever the subject, if a good teacher can inspire you and hold your attention, then you'll learn! Now I'm not a teacher but the system I've used in previous publications on Amazon seems to work well, particularly with children.

This edition includes a selection of those "WoW" facts combined with some pretty awesome pictures, if I say so myself! At the end there is a short "True or False" quiz to check memory recall and to help cement some of the information included in the book. Don't worry though, it's a bit of fun but at the same time, it helps to check your understanding.

Please note that if you're an expert on this subject then you may not find anything new here. If however you enjoy hearing sensational and extraordinary trivia and you like looking at some great pictures then I think you'll love it.

Matt.

In true Matthew Harper tradition, I thought that before we get down to some of those amazing aircraft facts, we might begin with some snapshots of a few of the different types, just to get the juices flowing..............

MIRAGE 2000

Image Courtesy of Airwolfhound

GULFSTREAM G650

Image Courtesy of charlywkarl

F-4 PHANTOM

Image Courtesy of Bundeswehr-Fotos Wir.Dienen.Deutschland

SPITFIRE

Image Courtesy of WillzUK

AIRBUS A320

MiG 15

Image Courtesy of Armchair Aviator

BOEING 747

Image Courtesy of Guimo

F-15C EAGLE

STEALTH BOMBER

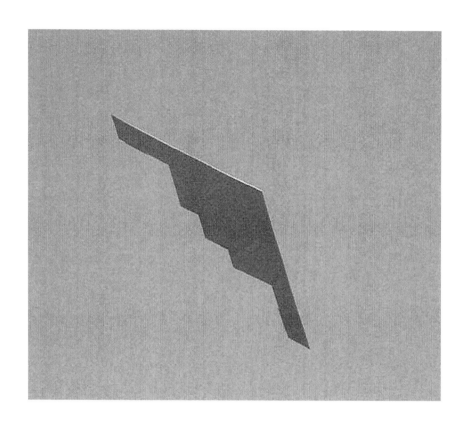

CONCORDE

Okay. Hope that helped to get you in the mood.

HERE WE GO..

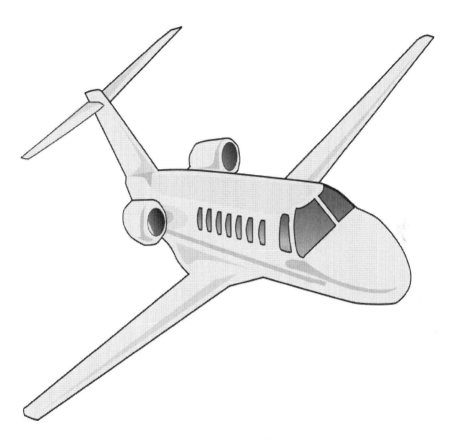

Image Courtesy of Jarno

Did you know that every 3 seconds, somewhere in the world, a plane is landing?

Image Courtesy of Sky Eckstrom

Did you know that the Wright brothers, (Orville & Wilbur), were credited with inventing and building the world's first successful plane?

Did you know that a Boeing 747 is made up of 6 million parts?

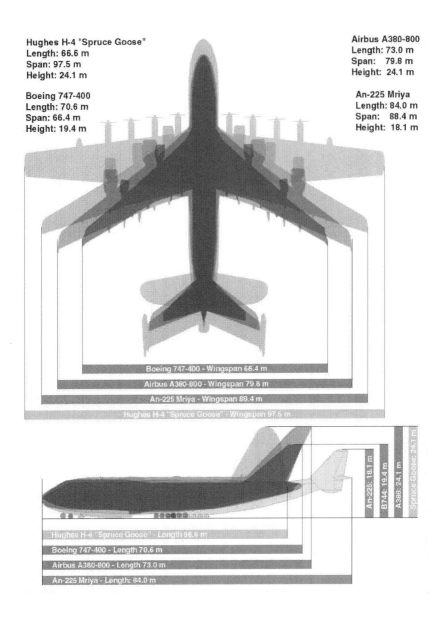

Hughes H-4 "Spruce Goose"
Length: 66.6 m
Span: 97.5 m
Height: 24.1 m

Boeing 747-400
Length: 70.6 m
Span: 66.4 m
Height: 19.4 m

Airbus A380-800
Length: 73.0 m
Span: 79.8 m
Height: 24.1 m

An-225 Mriya
Length: 84.0 m
Span: 88.4 m
Height: 18.1 m

Boeing 747-400 - Wingspan 66.4 m
Airbus A380-800 - Wingspan 79.8 m
An-225 Mriya - Wingspan 88.4 m
Hughes H-4 "Spruce Goose" - Wingspan 97.5 m

An-225: 18.1 m
B744: 19.4 m
A388: 24.1 m
Spruce Goose: 24.1 m

Hughes H-4 "Spruce Goose" - Length 66.6 m
Boeing 747-400 - Length 70.6 m
Airbus A380-800 - Length 73.0 m
An-225 Mriya - Length: 84.0 m

Did you know that the Havilland Comet was the first commercial airliner? It was built in 1949 in Great Britain.

Image Courtesy of InSapphoWeTrust

Did you know that only around 5% of people in the world have ever flown on a plane?

Image Courtesy of Lodian

Did you know that donkeys kill more people every year than plane crashes do?

Image Courtesy of farbe

Did you know that the American P-51D Mustang was introduced in 1944? It was the only Allied fighter in the Second World War that was capable of reaching distances of almost 2,000 miles without having to refuel.

Image Courtesy of pmarkham

Did you know that the Waco 10 was first introduced in 1927 and in the same year, accounted for 40% of all aircraft sold?

Image Courtesy of Armchair Aviator

Did you know that the U.S. Air Force's SR-71 Blackbird is currently the world's fastest jet reaching speeds of more than 2000 mph (Mach 3.5)?

Image Courtesy of foqus

Did you know that on 7th February 1996, Concorde became the fastest transatlantic airliner flying from New York to London in 2 hours, 52 minutes and 59 seconds?

Did you know that over 80% of people are afraid of flying?

Did you know that the Airbus A380 is currently the world's largest passenger airliner? It provides seating for 525 people using a standard 3-class configuration.

Image Courtesy of Steff, French Wikipedia (Clients A380.jpg)

Did you know that the Japanese "Mitsubishi Zero" was the first naval fighter plane able to outperform aircraft on land?

Image Courtesy of Armchair Aviator

Did you know that "Flying" is not the safest form of travel, it's actually the Bus?

Image Courtesy of wollebolleke

Did you know that the Hartsfield-Jackson International Airport in Atlanta is the busiest airport in the world? In 2012 it was visited by more than 95 million passengers.

Did you know that the F-4 Phantom held five speed records for 13 years?

Did you know that one engine on a Boeing 747 weighs nearly 9,500 pounds (4,300 kg)?

Did you know that the Bleriot XI was the first plane to cross the English Channel on 25th July, 1909? It took about 36 minutes.

Image Courtesy of HooLengSiong

Did you know that in 1986, the Rutan Voyager was the first aircraft to fly around the world without having to stop or refuel?

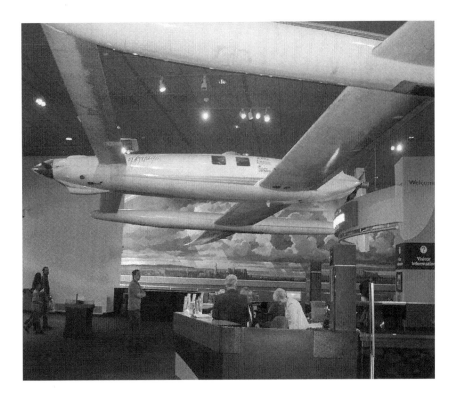

Did you know that the Supermarine Spitfire was the only British fighter in continuous production throughout the Second World War?

Image Courtesy of Smudge 9000

Did you know that the F-16 Fighting Falcon has a maximum speed of over Mach 2 and is able to pull 9G manoeuvres?

Did you know that even if you put on a pair of giant wings, you could never fly? The human heart is unable to pump the blood quickly enough to satisfy the vast amount of energy required to flap your arms at such a speed.

Image Courtesy of kablam

Did you know that the first twin turboprop aircraft produced specifically for corporate travel was the Gulfstream 1?

Did you know that the Extra 300 was a such a huge force in aerobatic manoeuvres that it was popularised in Microsoft's "Flight Simulator"?

Image Courtesy of Airwolfhound

Did you know that the Captain and the First Officer on a commercial aircraft are always instructed to eat different food from the menu in case of food poisoning?

Image Courtesy of AvgeekJoe

Did you know that the BAE Harrier was the first fighter able to land vertically?

Image Courtesy of I Wish I Was Flying

Did you know that the Hindenburg was the largest aircraft that ever flew? It was 245 m (803 ft 10 in) in length and had a diameter of 41.18 m (135.1 ft 0 in).

Did you know that the Bell X-1 was the first plane to go faster than the speed of sound in level flight?

Did you know that the Citation X is currently the fastest civil plane reaching speeds of up to Mac 0.92, (almost the speed of sound)?

Image Courtesy of Luccio.errera

Did you know that in 1986, David Childs set a world record with 2368 consecutive loops in a plane?

Image Courtesy of ankurdave

Did you know that the brakes on a jet aircraft can take up to 45 minutes to cool?

Image Courtesy of wbaiv

Did you know that the B-2 bomber (Stealth Bomber) is by far the most expensive military plane with a price tag of $2.4 billion?

Did you know that since 1940, the airline industry has made a loss of over $30 billion dollars?

Image Courtesy of johnpwarren

Did you know that the Airbus A340 is powered by 4 Rolls Royce Trent engines?

Image Courtesy of My name

Did you know that the Hawker Hurricane was responsible for 60% of the Royal Air Force victories in battle?

Did you know that the Boeing 747-400 has 4 landing gear? Three main and one extra at the nose.

Image Courtesy of AvgeekJoe

Did you know that the F-4 Phantom II was nicknamed "Rhino" or "Double Ugly" by the Americans?

Did you know that the F-111 was the first aircraft in production to use variable-sweep wing technology? This allowed the wings to sweep back and then return to their original position during flight.

Did you know that the Hughes H-4 Hercules, (nicknamed the "Spruce Goose"), only ever flew once in 1947, was made almost entirely out of birch wood and had the largest wingspan of any aircraft ever made?

Did you know that "Memphis Belle" was the nickname given to one of the first B-17 heavy bombers to complete 25 combat missions with all her crew alive in World War II?

Image Courtesy of marada

Did you know that the B-1A used a crew escape capsule that ejected as a complete unit? This was because normal ejection at high speed could be fatal.

Did you know that any aircraft flown by the Air Force that is carrying the President of the U.S.A. is called Air Force One? Once the President has left the aircraft, it reverts back to its original name.

Did you know that the Boeing B-52 is known as BUFF which stands for Big Ugly Fat Fellow.

Did you know that "Ball Lightening" can form inside a plane and can appear to roll down the aisle whilst glowing?

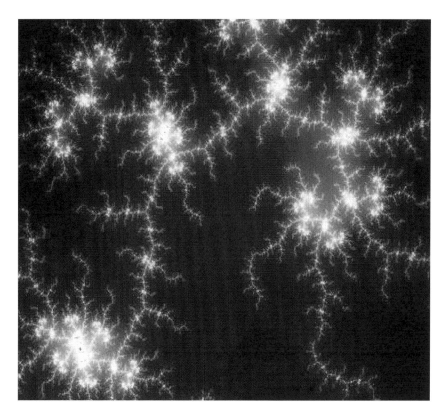

Image Courtesy of Dumb Scientist

Did you know that the Douglas SBD Dauntless only had one engine?

Did you know that the NASA X-43 is the fastest aircraft (unmanned) on record reaching speeds of around 7000 m.p.h. (10,460 km/h)?

Did you know that the Denney Kitfox was one of the first small, personal kit aircraft to be produced? Initial designs featured a quickly folding wing allowing for easy transportation and storage.

Did you know that Prince Alwaleed bin Talal from Saudi Arabia bought himself an Airbus 380 for over $300 million?

Did you know that the Antonov An-225 Mriya is the largest and heaviest operational aircraft in the world?

Image Courtesy of Dmitry A. Mottl

Did you know that the Space Shuttle reached speeds of up to 17,500 miles per hour? This book is dedicated to the brave men and women who tragically lost their lives aboard Columbia & Challenger.

That's about it for the trivia for now. I'd like to finish this publication with TEN "True or False" questions based on what you've just read. It should help you to really cement the information and to test your memory recall!

....

....

DON'T FORGET TO KEEP YOUR SCORE: THERE'S 1 POINT FOR EACH OF THE FIRST 9 QUESTIONS AND 5 POINTS FOR THE BONUS QUESTION GIVING A TOTAL OF 14 POINTS ....

1.

TRUE or FALSE: Every 6 seconds, somewhere in the world, a plane is landing.

FALSE

Every **3** seconds, somewhere in the world, a plane is landing.

2.

TRUE or FALSE: A Boeing 747 is made up of 6 million parts.

TRUE

3.

TRUE or FALSE: Monkeys kill more people every year than plane crashes do.

FALSE

DONKEYS kill more people every year than plane crashes do.

4.

TRUE or FALSE: Flying is the safest form of travel.

FALSE

Flying is not the safest form of travel, it's actually the **BUS**.

5.

TRUE or FALSE: The Bleriot XI was the first plane to cross the English Channel on 25th July, 1909? It took about 36 minutes.

TRUE

6.

TRUE or FALSE: The BAE Harrier was the first fighter able to land vertically.

TRUE

7.

TRUE or FALSE: In 1986, David Childs set a world record with 2368 consecutive barrel rolls in a plane.

FALSE

In 1986, David Childs set a world record with 2368 consecutive LOOPS in a plane.

8.

TRUE or FALSE: The Boeing 747-400 has 4 landing gear? Three main and one extra at the nose.

TRUE

9.

TRUE or FALSE: "Miami Belle" was the nickname given to one of the first B-17 heavy bombers to complete 25 combat missions with all her crew alive in World War II

FALSE

"**MEMPHIS** Belle" was the nickname given to one of the first B-17 heavy bombers to complete 25 combat missions with all her crew alive in World War II.

10.

BONUS ROUND WORTH 5 POINTS

TRUE or FALSE: Prince Alwaleed bin Talal from Saudi Arabia bought himself a bus for over $300 million.

FALSE

Prince Alwaleed bin Talal from Saudi Arabia bought himself an **AIRBUS 380** for over $300 million.

Congratulations, you made it to the end!

I sincerely hope you enjoyed my little aircraft project and that you learnt a thing or two. I certainly did when I was doing the research.

ADD UP YOUR SCORE NOW.

1 point for each of the first 9 correct answers plus 5 points for the bonus round giving a grand total of 14 points.

If you genuinely achieved 14 points then you are indeed a

"**JET MASTER**".

8 to 13 points proves you are a "**JET LEGEND**".

4 to 7 points shows you are a "**JET ENTHUSIAST**".

0 to 3 points shows you are a "**JET ADMIRER**".

NICE WORK!

Matt.

Thank you once again for choosing this publication. If you enjoyed it then please let me know using the Customer Review Section through Amazon.

If you would like to read more of my work then simply type in my name using the Amazon Search Box and hopefully you'll find something else that "takes your fancy" or go directly to my website printed below.

Until we meet again,

Matthew Harper

www.matthewharper.info

108

33453595R00063

Printed in Poland
by Amazon Fulfillment
Poland Sp. z o.o., Wrocław